Michelanne Forster is a native Californian who immigrated to New Zealand in 1973. She directs childrens programmes for Television New Zealand as well as writing plays and books. Her previously published books for children are *Rodney Rat and the Sunken Treasure* and *The Four Legged Prince*.

Graeme Kyle is third in a family of four children born and raised in Nelson. After graduating from the University of Canterbury School of Fine Art he worked for Television New Zealand. He now works as a freelance illustrator based in Nelson. He has illustrated *The Play School Book, The Wildtrack Book, The Second Big Play School Book, The Four Legged Prince* and *Taniwha: The Monster Book for New Zealand Children*.

Rodney Rat

and
the Sneaky Weasel Gang

by Michelanne Forster and Graeme Kyle

HODDER AND STOUGHTON

AUCKLAND LONDON SYDNEY TORONTO

Text copyright © 1986 Michelanne Forster
Illustrations © Graeme Kyle
First published 1986
ISBN 0 340 379243

Typeset by Auckland TypoGraphic Services Ltd.
Printed and bound in Hong Kong for Hodder & Stoughton Ltd,
46 View Road, Glenfield, Auckland 10, New Zealand.

One day Rodney Rat found a ring at the rubbish tip. It had a ruby-red stone that sparkled. He was polishing his new-found treasure when ...
RATTLE, RATTLE, CLUNK! A tin landed at his feet.

The tin was full of pebbles – and a slightly sticky note. It said, 'Watch Out For Us!' Signed, The Sneaky Weasel Gang.

Rodney looked up and saw three weasels sitting in an old Zephyr Six. They were wearing tee-shirts and dark glasses.

The weasels got out of the car and walked over to Rodney. Then they played a trick on him. Two of the weasels pointed excitedly at the sky. Then the biggest weasel grabbed the ruby ring and ran!

Rodney chased the Sneaky Weasel Gang into the bush but he couldn't catch them. He didn't think the trick they'd played on him was at all funny.

Maybe his friends would help him. But when Rodney went to see the other rats they were busy watching television. Besides, the Sneaky Weasel Gang sounded scary.

Rodney was determined to get his ring back. He packed a rucksack with a bottle of water, cheese, a compass, a map, a rope, a torch and a Special Disguise Kit. Then he put an explorer's whistle around his neck. The other rats thought he was crazy.

Rodney followed the Sneaky Weasel Gang's footprints into the bush. The further he went from the rubbish tip, the more frightened he became.

The sun went down and the moon came up. Rodney
began to imagine all kinds of creepy things.

Meanwhile, the other rats began to worry about Rodney.
Even though they didn't like the dark, they put parkas
on over their pyjamas and went out to look for him.

But Rodney was already into the heart of the bush. He had spotted a camp fire on the other side of a big river. It was much too swift to cross so he made a rope bridge and crossed the water hand over hand.

When he reached the other side he heard voices. Rodney crept towards them. It was the Sneaky Weasel Gang! They were toasting marshmallows, and the biggest weasel was wearing the ruby ring on his head like a crown.

Rodney took the Special Disguise Kit out of his rucksack and strapped it on. He looked so much like a tree fern that the weasels didn't notice him creeping closer and closer. Just as he was about to snatch the ring back ...

REOW!!! A wild cat leapt out of the bush! The weasels shrieked and ran into their hide-out. Rodney tried to follow them but they slammed the door in his face.

The wild cat pinned Rodney down with one paw.
Then she stuck her other paw through the window and
hooked the biggest weasel by his tee-shirt. The weasel
cried out and kicked but he couldn't get away.

Rodney was so scared his whiskers wilted. But he knew he had to do something! Just as the cat was about to pop the weasel in her mouth, Rodney grabbed his explorer's whistle. He blew it with all his might!

EEEEEEEEK!!! The whistle shrilled and the cat sprang into the air. She let go of the weasel in fright and ran away.

The weasels were so grateful they rushed up to Rodney and hugged him. Then the biggest weasel picked up the ruby ring and placed it on Rodney's head.

Suddenly the other rats burst into the clearing. They had found Rodney at last!

The weasels invited all the rats to a party in Rodney's honour. They danced and ate chips and cheese, sausage rolls and cheese, jelly and ice-cream and cheese, and just plain cheese.

When the party was over the weasels gave Rodney a special SNEAKY tee-shirt. Then the other rats put Rodney on their shoulders, and carried him home to bed.

The End